Learning to Laugh at Work

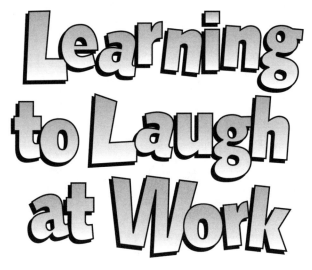

Learning to Laugh at Work

The Power of Humor in the Workplace

Robert McGraw

SkillPath Publications
Mission, Kansas

Project Editor: Kelly Scanlon

Editor: Jane Doyle Guthrie

Cover and Book Design: Rod Hankins

Library of Congress Catalog Card Number: 95-70451

ISBN: 1-878542-40-0

10 9 8   04

Printed in the United States of America

Contents

Introduction

In 1981, as President Ronald Reagan was rushed to the hospital with a life-threatening chest wound, the people of the world watched the ensuing events carefully. The death of a nation's leader can affect international economies, security, and morale. But the President demonstrated that his reputation for wit was well deserved. In spite of his injuries, he used his sense of humor to put others at ease. While being wheeled into the operating room, he smiled up at the surgeons and quipped, "Please assure me that you are all good Republicans." A few hours after the operation he felt well enough to send a note to his White House staff. "If I had had this much attention in Hollywood," he wrote, "I would have stayed there."

Do you steer away from humor on the job? Are you afraid people will think you aren't serious about business? Do you fear that your attempts at humor might backfire?

Wit in the workplace doesn't mean memorizing jokes or acting like a clown. Successful business people know that humor, when used effectively and appropriately, is a valuable management tool. In fact, it could easily be called one of the keys to leadership success.

Your sense of humor can help you whether you're trying to climb the career ladder or be happy right where you are. The skillful use of humor can disarm your adversaries, increase your authority and charisma, and make you a valuable and appreciated colleague.

As you read and work through the exercises that follow, you'll:

- Learn how humor can put an appealing polish on your professional presence.

- Win the respect of your co-workers and develop the confidence that comes from knowing how to put other people at ease.

- Possibly improve your overall health (some medical experts say laughter offers many health benefits).

In short, this book will help you claim all the advantages that come from learning to laugh—at home, at play, *and* at work.

Chapter One

A Potent Form of Communication

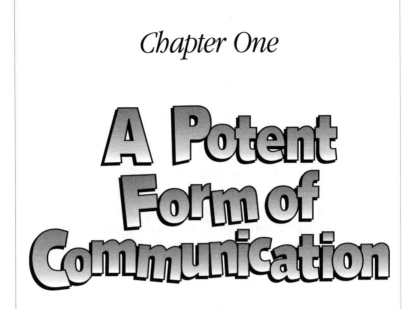

When comedian Bob Hope was meeting with his writers one day, he told them he needed some new football jokes for an upcoming appearance at Notre Dame. "But, Bob," one of them said, "we've been writing football jokes for you for months. You can't possibly have used all of them. Why do you want new jokes?"

Hope turned to the writer and quipped, "I pay you with new money, don't I?"

The writer got the point.

"Getting the point" is at the bottom line of everything in business. Success in the workplace requires a high degree of skill in communicating with other people. Goals, strategies, objectives, rules, procedures, techniques, results—all require a successful communication process. When someone "gets the point," our efforts to communicate have been effective.

But getting the point doesn't mean all communication has to be pointed. Being tough with others may seem to get immediate results, but it also can set the stage for bigger and more unpleasant problems somewhere in the future, when the people you were needlessly tough with seize an opportunity for "pay-back time."

The friendly approach gets the job done faster, more effectively, and without negative repercussions. As the old saying goes, "Softly, softly, catchee monkey." Here's where humor is invaluable. Bob Hope could have played the part of the tough-as-nails boss and said, "Either write some new jokes by tomorrow, or you're fired!" That certainly would have put his point across. But he knew better. In addition to being a great performer, Bob Hope is a highly successful businessman who understands that the key to effective management is the ability to win people to your side. So he handled the situation with humor. He didn't hurt anyone's feelings, he didn't make an enemy, yet he got the result he wanted.

Taking yourself less seriously can be a real asset to your career. According to some executive recruiters, seven out of ten people who are fired lose their jobs because of personality conflicts, not lack of skill.

Lee Iacocca agrees. Quoted in *Gender Quotes,* he says: "The major reason capable people fail to advance is that they don't work well with their colleagues. The statement, 'He's good, but he had trouble getting along with other people,' is the kiss of death for management potential...The key to success is not information. It's people."

The skillful and appropriate use of humor is one of the hallmarks of effective leadership. When you use humor skillfully and appropriately, it demonstrates these traits:

- You have self-confidence.

- You feel in control of the situation.

- You are comfortable with yourself.

Knowing when and how to banter, quip, tell a joke, or just lighten the atmosphere will set you head and shoulders above the majority who lack self-confidence and people skills.

Getting the point also means understanding things yourself, especially priorities. As a businessperson, your main priorities involve pleasing other people: customers, clients, co-workers, and management. But you must also put a high priority on making yourself happy in your career. No one wants to go through life saying "this job just isn't worth the hassle."

Having good business sense should include developing a good business sense of humor. Humor can help you overcome a multitude of problems and situations that might otherwise discourage you, depress you, or even make you ill. If you think "success" is worth making yourself or others miserable, then you've missed an important point in life.

Marine biologists tell us that when fish are in trouble, they send distress signals out through the water. Unfortunately for the fish, these signals actually attract their enemies, the sharks. When you're frustrated and stressed, you unconsciously communicate these feelings, and other people sense them. Those around you at work may begin to lose confidence in your ability to overcome difficulties, handle certain situations, and provide competent leadership. Your charisma is weakened and you begin to "leak power." If you allow this to happen, you may suddenly find that you have become just another poor fish, in distress and swimming with the sharks.

Being able to see the light side of problems not only helps you survive, it also shows others that you have self-confidence and the ability to stay "centered" and keep your priorities straight in spite of difficulties. Colleagues will trust you and trust your judgment—people naturally follow a confident leader.

More important than that, you will be a happier person. In his book *The Healing Power of Humor,* Allen Klein writes: "In laughter, we transcend our predicaments. We are lifted above our feelings of fear, discouragement, and despair. People who can laugh at their setbacks no longer feel sorry for themselves. They feel uplifted, encouraged, and empowered."

In the following pages, you'll learn what humor is, and how and when humor should (and shouldn't) be used in business settings. Study this book and do the exercises, and you'll find yourself gradually becoming:

- Less stressed out.

- More self-confident.

- Better able to communicate ideas and desires to others without antagonizing them.

- More likely to inspire others' confidence and win them to your point of view.

- Generally nicer to be around.

By the time you finish reading, you'll agree that trying to be a success in business without developing a sense of humor is not only very difficult, it's downright pointless. On the other hand, becoming a happy, productive individual who helps others become happy and productive is a pretty good definition of success, by any standards.

Get the point?

EXERCISE #1

Evaluating Your Business Wit

Before getting into specific issues and techniques, engage in a little self-reflection and analyze your business sense of humor. Answer "yes" or "no" to the following questions:

Yes   No

☐   ☐   1. Do you feel business should be serious and that managers should set the example by avoiding humor?

☐   ☐   2. Does it bother you when other people laugh in business situations?

☐   ☐   3. Do you lack self-confidence, especially when you're with people who are higher on the business ladder than you?

☐   ☐   4. Do you think people in business who laugh and have fun are probably not doing their jobs very well?

☐   ☐   5. In business situations, are you embarrassed to laugh because you're afraid someone else won't think the same thing is funny?

☐   ☐   6. Do you think a little sexy teasing and joking is okay once in a while, just as long as no one in the office actually complains?

☐   ☐   7. Do you think people ought to be able to handle it when you make a good-natured insult or put-down, provided you didn't really mean any harm by it?

☐ ☐ 8. When you make a mistake in front of your co-workers, do you lash back with a caustic remark or spend hours cursing yourself for letting them see that you aren't perfect?

☐ ☐ 9. Do you think a good way to be witty and humorous is to memorize jokes from *Reader's Digest* or *Playboy?*

☐ ☐ 10. Do you find that your attempts at humor often fall flat?

For every "yes," give yourself one lash with a wet noodle and resolve to read this book at least twice. For every "no," give yourself a pat on the back and say: "I can do this! I'm already on the way."

Chapter Two

Fears and Fallacies

Probably as a carryover from childhood, when we were scolded for giggling in church or snickering during class, most of us have the idea that "important" situations are no place to have funny thoughts. It's not hard to understand, then, where that little voice comes from that tells you not to be "silly" at work—serious business calls for a serious attitude, right?

Well, not exactly. The key is to show *appropriate* reactions. Sometimes a little levity moves a group or a moment along better than a lot of seriousness does. To get comfortable with this notion, let's expose some fallacies (and maybe some of your fears) about humor on the job.

1. **Humor isn't appropriate in business.** *People will think I'm wasting time. We're too busy for humor.* Wrong. Being humorous doesn't mean we don't take our jobs seriously enough, it just means we don't take *ourselves* too seriously. It means we have our priorities straight. One good way to keep your priorities straight

is to make a place on your desk or workstation for a picture frame that's labeled "What I'm Working For." In this frame should be a photo of the person or people you love. Everyone in business should have such a reminder.

Lighthearted doesn't mean frivolous. Humor simply helps us remember what should be the real bottom line of all our business endeavors: People are more important than things. Business is not exclusively about selling products, supplying services, or building a better widget; it's also about people and relationships and being of benefit to others.

2. **Being humorous will undermine my authority.**
People will think I don't know how to "take charge."
False. Used properly, humor actually strengthens your
aura of confidence, control, and authority. (This will be
discussed in more detail later.) Humor is a way of
regulating the *tone* of a relationship. Being funny
doesn't decrease your leadership; it enhances it. If you
are controlling the tone of the situation, you are the
leader in that situation, regardless of your title or job
description.

And speaking of leaders, do you know who gave (and
practiced) the following advice? "You cannot deal with
the most serious things in the world unless you also
understand the most amusing." It was Sir Winston
Churchill, a leader who kept his sense of humor, and
kept the world inspired, throughout the darkest days of
World War II.

3. **Some people just aren't funny and they shouldn't
try.** *People won't think I'm funny. I'll "bomb."* Untrue.
People who aren't naturally humorous have even more
reason to work on developing their technique. Being
funny is an ability, and a valuable one, that can be
learned. Others have developed their humor skills, and
you can too. You already have the first and most
important qualification—desire—or you wouldn't be
reading this book.

4. **Being humorous keeps people from being successful.** *People will think I'm just a clown, a loser.* Not so. Look at the successful people around you—probably 90 percent of them have a good, healthy sense of humor. An understanding of the value of humor is evident in successful people with such widely varied backgrounds as consultant Stephen Covey, author Robert Townsend, former auto executive Lee Iacocca, television host Deborah Norville, former Texas governor Ann Richards, journalist Ellen Goodman ... well, the complete list would take an entire book.

Learning to See Humor in Situations

To help you develop the knack of "seeing things funny," write down a parody version of something familiar. Here are some ideas to get you started:

- Television commercials

  Example: A commercial with the McDonald's slogan "Have you had your break today?" could show convicts eating hamburgers while digging a tunnel under the prison wall.

- Ads or PR materials

  Example: A billboard might read, "The Marine Corps—All we need are a few good men (and a hundred billion dollars a year)."

- Famous people's names

  Example: Some critics called former President Reagan "Ronald Ray-gun" because of the "Star Wars" missile defense system.

- Well-known songs

  Example: Instead of "I Left My Heart in San Francisco," try singing "I left my fat at the Mayo Clinic."

If these categories don't stimulate your imagination, try movie titles, road signs, or well-known business mottoes.

Write your parody here.

_____

_____

_____

_____

_____

_____

_____

_____

_____

_____

_____

_____

_____

_____

_____

_____

_____

Chapter Three

...and Fundamental Benefits

Now that you've loosened up your thinking a little and perhaps challenged a few myths about mirth, let's shift the focus to humor's strong points in the workplace. There are some significant benefits you should be aware of.

1. **Humor bonds teams.** Humor is effective in establishing the sense of group identity and togetherness that welds a collection of individuals into a team. It also helps break down the sense of distance that occurs naturally between managers and those they supervise. Research shows that when two or more people feel comfortable making jokes to or even about each other, they develop a feeling of mutual trust, respect, and confidence. The group in effect creates a bond—a humor/trust circle—that pulls the members closer together and cements the team relationship. Humor keeps people willing to work together. In an atmosphere of humor, trust, and mutual goodwill, they don't feel threatened so easily.

When workers consider their supervisor to be "part of the team," that manager's authority is not diminished—it actually increases. Team members feel that since the manager is "one of us," he or she can be trusted to make decisions that won't be harmful to the welfare of the group as a whole or to individual members.

Bosses who don't make the effort to put themselves inside the humor/trust circle fall into one of two categories:

- Arrogant/competent

- Benevolent/incompetent

The arrogant/competent supervisor is not generally liked by the team. Often the relationship between this manager and team members is autocratic or even confrontational. There may be obedience, but there is no loyalty. Workers in this situation often perform only the minimum requirements in order to keep their jobs.

Under this type of supervision, employees have no emotional "buy-in" to the goals and standards of the company; they simply put in their hours. Serious problems may surface such as absenteeism, abuse or sabotage of equipment, friction between employees, abuse of privileges, or petty theft of supplies. Even certain instances of workplace violence can have roots in a poor relationship between workers and an authoritarian supervisor.

The other kind of boss outside the humor/trust circle falls into the category of "benevolent but incompetent." This sort of manager often becomes the object of the group's humor, but only behind his or her back. Poking fun at the boss may strengthen group unity a little, but the overall effect is negative. Most of us are uncomfortable with the practice of ridiculing other people in secret. "If that's what they say when the boss isn't around, I wonder what they say about *me* when I'm not here."

In addition, this type of ridicule hurts the manager/team relationship, a relationship that must be as strong and as comfortable as possible for the department or business unit to thrive. Here again, serious problems may arise.

Once team spirit has been established, humor still serves a valuable purpose. A team that enjoys the work and each other's company is more likely to be willing to take on new, even more demanding assignments, plus members can be productive when they don't particularly like the task. Even pulling weeds doesn't seem so bad when you're doing it with a group of people who are "all in the same boat." In situations like this, we unconsciously try to ease each other's burden by making light of the hardships involved in the task and by emphasizing the enjoyable moments.

In business, an effective supervisor works to achieve this kind of group dynamics: everyone sharing the good and putting up with a few inconveniences in order to reach a common goal. Team spirit, group loyalty, esprit de corps—whatever else you want to call it—is a selfless and often enthusiastic devotion to the group and its purposes.

Here's a way to create opportunities for laughter to ring out at work. Before a staff meeting, ask everyone to write down and bring a favorite joke or one clipped from a magazine (perhaps about your industry or profession).

At the beginning of the meeting, put the jokes into a container, stir them up, and have someone select three to read aloud (anonymously). The joke that gets the biggest laugh wins $3. Second place gets $2, and third place, $1. This way the meeting begins with a relaxed atmosphere of humor and mutual trust. Later, when the heavy issues come up, people are more likely to cooperate because they have that reservoir of goodwill to fall back on.

As a variation, instead of jokes, you could ask for the funniest (or dumbest) thing a customer or co-worker ever did (no names, please!), or invite people to submit something funny they or a member of their family once did. (It's all voluntary; no pressure on anyone.) This sort of sharing of "dubious deeds" could also become a humorous column in your company newsletter.

2. **Humor conveys authority.** The wise use of humor offers an excellent way to demonstrate self-confidence. That's a vital attribute that you want to convey subtly to others, so don't be afraid to poke a little fun at yourself occasionally.

   Self-deprecating humor is a powerful leadership tool. It serves to bridge the communication gap between you and your co-workers, especially those you supervise. When you laugh at your own weaknesses, it makes others feel that your shortcomings can't really be very serious faults. Self-effacing humor defuses potential areas of criticism, making it harder for people to find fault with you and easier for them to agree with you.

3. **Humor reduces stress.** Laughing stimulates the release of endorphins, the painkilling chemicals in the brain similar to morphine. Instead of the old cliché, "It only hurts when I laugh," we should actually say, "It only stops hurting when I laugh." In his book *Anatomy of an Illness,* Norman Cousins wrote that ten minutes of laughter "has the same anesthetic effect of at least two hours of pain-free sleep."

   Endorphins give us a sense of well-being and confidence, and can help us handle stress better, but there are other health benefits in laughter as well. Blood circulation increases, heartbeat rises, muscles release tension, and the endocrine system is stimulated. Laughing may also strengthen the immune system. Even a little smile can help. Some scientists believe that smiling changes the relative tension of certain muscles in the jaw and the back of the neck, which in turn triggers the endorphins.

4. Humor helps us keep problems in perspective. Wit is a way of looking at life, a way of perceiving what's happening around us. Humor presents no more or less a reality than any other emotion, but it's a great way of *dealing* with reality. It helps us through the difficulties in life. Will Rogers and Eddie Cantor made fortunes during the Depression because people needed to laugh in order to handle those very tough times.

Today, political humorists such as Mark Russell and Art Buchwald help us laugh about taxes, regulations, and the people we elect to represent us. Erma Bombeck keeps us in stitches about the trials of family life, and Phyllis Diller's running gags about her plastic surgery have more than paid for all her surgical stitches.

In short, laughter:

- Keeps you from moping.
- Helps you start hoping.
- Leads you toward coping.

Turning Clichés Into Potent One-Liners

Audiences love David Letterman's satirical Top Ten lists, partly because newspapers have printed Top Ten lists so often that the idea has become a cliché.

Clichés can be funny, especially if you really push them to the point of absurdity. Instead of saying, "He looked like something

the cat dragged in," say, "He looked like something the cat refused to drag in." Or, "He looked like something the cat dragged in to scare the mice." Or, "He looked like something the cat coughed up."

Complete the following clichés with your own original ideas.

1. If at first you don't succeed, _____

_____

_____ .

2. She was as mad as a _____

_____

_____ .

3. It was raining_____

and _____ .

4. A penny saved is_____

_____

_____ .

5. A stitch in time _____

_____

_____ .

6. Early to bed and early to rise _____

_____

_____ .

7. A _____ a day keeps the

_____ away.

8. His face was as red as a _____

_____ .

Add your own cliché variations here:

9. _____

_____

_____ .

10. _____

_____

_____ .

11. _____

_____

_____ .

12. _____

_____

_____ .

13. _____

_____

_____ .

Chapter Four

The Building Blocks of Humor

Like many things in life, there are certain principles and techniques that make humor work. Learning and practicing them won't necessarily turn you into David Letterman, but you can definitely gain some understanding of what makes things funny. And that will go a long way toward helping you develop the skill of making others laugh.

The Setup and the Punch Line

First among the basic forms and devices of humor are the *setup* and the *punch line*. The whole concept of humor can be summed up in two words: "Surprise, surprise!" Humor's main characteristic is incongruity—the clash between the way we expect something to be and the way it actually turns out. Humor springs from contrast and depends on the balance between tension and release.

Sometimes the setup is only a few words; other times it may take a few sentences. There is a practical limit, however, to how long a joke can drag out without spoiling the surprise and the humor. As a general rule, if the punch line doesn't come by the fourth or fifth line, there's a good chance you won't get much of a laugh. If the punch line doesn't come until the tenth or twelfth line, you may not hear anything at all except the echo of an empty room. "Brevity is the soul of wit," wrote Shakespeare, and he's been making audiences happy for four hundred years.

There's a rhythm to humor, just as there is in music, and one of the best combinations is something called *the triple*—essentially a setup, another setup, and then a punch line. (A musician would call this an AAB form.) The punch line is funny because we've been led down the primrose path (twice, no less) by relatively mundane statements. We have been lulled into expecting that the next (the third) statement will be equally ho-hum. Instead, it is incongruous, often wildly so. It is this contrasting element (the "old switcheroo") that is surprising and elicits the laugh:

> "OK, here's my agenda for this morning. First I'll stack the good letters on the left and the complaint letters on the right. Then I'll read the one good letter. Then I'll look at the stack of two hundred complaints and jump out the nearest window."

See how it works?

(A)   I'll stack the good letters … (ho-hum)

(A)   I'll read the one good letter … (ho-hum)

(B)   I'll jump out the nearest window (say WHAT?!)

Listen for ten minutes to any humorist of any style from any time period, and you're almost guaranteed to hear at least one "triple" (although they are often more subtle than the example above).

Milking a joke, another common technique, is essentially an add-on method for getting your listeners on a "laugh roll." You can build on a punch line by adding a second or even a third punch line relating to the original idea. (Listen to some of Bill Cosby's solo routines; he's a master at pushing a comic situation to the brink.)

Let's see how you might build on the idea that was used in the "triple" about the stack of complaint letters:

> "OK, here's my agenda for this morning. First I'll stack the good letters on the left and the complaint letters on the right. Then I'll read the one good letter. Then I'll take the two hundred complaints and throw them out the nearest window."

Now push the idea:

> "Better yet, I'll shred the letters first. If someone sees me throwing them out, I can say I thought I heard a parade going by."

Now push it further:

> "My desk will be clear and it won't even be coffee break time—this could get me a raise *and* a promotion."

Push some more:

> "Now I've got time to take the good letter, make two hundred copies, and forge phony names on each one. By lunch time, I'll have the best-looking file of letters in the company."

Well, be careful not to push it *too* far!

The Call-Back

Another device used in humor is the *call-back*—a reference to something mentioned previously in the routine. Each time the original idea is "called back," we remember that it was associated with pleasure (humor) before. This puts us in a more relaxed, receptive mood.

David Letterman will often catch something at the beginning of a show, such as the bandleader's or an audience member's comments, and keep calling it back throughout the program. Eventually, he can turn an otherwise mundane remark into a running gag that gets laughs even though it originally wasn't funny.

Often a tangible object can be turned into a visual running gag that provokes chuckles even it it's only touched or picked up. Judy Tenuta's accordian is an example of a visual call-back, as was the violin in the hands of Henny Youngman or Jack Benny.

Jack Benny picking up his violin, for example, was sure to get a laugh because audiences had been reminded time after time, over many years, that he played the instrument so terribly it was downright funny. (The truth is, he actually played quite well and often soloed with symphony orchestras at charity benefit concerts.)

Exaggeration

The technique of *exaggeration* can often boost ordinary things into something funny. Don't be afraid to push an idea to the limit—and then some.

Dull: "I turned around and faced a big policeman. And he said …"

Better: "I turned around and faced a policeman the size of a Mack truck. And he said …"

Funny: "Then I noticed a big shadow come over me and I thought we were having an eclipse. So I turned around and here I am, looking up at a policeman the size of Mount Rushmore. And just as solid. I could even see the chisel marks in his face!

"When he opened his mouth, pebbles rolled down his chin. I could see some poor climber's rope still caught between his front teeth. And he said ..."

Saying the policeman is the size of Mount Rushmore is a mildly humorous exaggeration. It's the sort of line Woody Allen and Bill Cosby often use. But skilled humorists like them wouldn't stop there, and neither should you. Build on the first exaggeration by saying that the cop is as solid as granite and still has the chisel marks to prove it. Then push the comparison even further with the image of pebbles rolling down his stony face.

When you use exaggeration, don't overdo it ("I've told you a hundred billion times, never exaggerate"). Trying too hard to get a laugh will almost always defeat the purpose. A policeman "the size of Mount Rushmore" may evoke a smile, but "I was looking at a policeman who was bigger than the moon!" is just plain juvenile. Good timing, controlled exaggeration, and practice will often let you milk extra laughs out of an idea that is only moderately funny to begin with.

Identification

Identification is another building block of humor. You've no doubt noticed that we become more upset when we read that a person we know was hurt than when we read that a hundred were injured in some other country. The same is true of humor: People enjoy humor more when they can relate to it. The more we identify, the more we chuckle. To help your listener identify with your humor, remember these three tools:

• Personalize

• Localize

• Empathize

Comedians Jerry Seinfeld and David Brenner, for example, are masters at drawing audiences this way. Both can put a hilarious spin on the frustrations and absurdities we all experience every day—trying to order carry-out food, forgetting where you parked the car at the mall, or whatever. Here's how it works:

Dull: "It seems one time there was this old lady yelling at a man in a department store. She said, 'What do you think ...' "

Better: "Last week I was in the department store and I saw an old lady yelling at a man. She said, 'What do you think ...' "

Funny: Last week I took my grandmother to K-Mart. She's a great lady; I love her. But a boy, can she get tough. She grabs me and starts yelling, 'What do you think ...' "

With the first example, you probably thought, "Ho-hum, here comes another gag lifted from *Reader's Digest*. There was no real connection between you and the people in the story. The second example was better, but not much. The last example was more likely to catch your interest because:

- *The setup was subtle.* You didn't recognize a joke was coming. When something seems like it might really have happened, it's much funnier than when we know it's just a joke.

- *It was personalized.* You know the person involved; you're standing there looking at me.

- *It was localized.* You're familiar with K-Mart and can probably picture being in one.

- *You could empathize.* Perhaps the setup reminded you of your own grandmother, or if not, you have probably known (or at least can imagine) a sweet older woman who can be tough when she needs to be. You may even have been yelled at in public before, too, and can empathize on that level as well.

Self-Deprecating Humor

A third fundamental technique, *self-deprecating humor,* can be thought of as the "gentle art of putting others at ease." When Ronald Reagan ran for President, his opponents tried to turn his age into a negative factor. Reagan defused the issue by making light of his age every chance he got. While addressing the Washington Press Club, for example, he mentioned that the club was founded in 1919, and then added, "It seems like only yesterday." Later he quoted Thomas Jefferson's advice not to worry about one's age and said, "And ever since he told me that, I stopped worrying." When opponent Walter Mondale accused him of government by amnesia, Reagan retorted, "I thought the remark accusing me of government by amnesia was uncalled for. And I wish I could remember who said it."

Many professional humorists—such as Joan Rivers, Erma Bombeck, and Richard Lewis—have parlayed this technique into popularity and success. Rodney Dangerfield's basic theme is "I don't get no respect." Jack Benny built his career around being a cheapskate. In one of his most famous skits, a robber pointed a gun at Benny and said, "Your money or your life!" For a very long moment, Benny just stood there. Finally, the gunman repeated, "I said, 'your money or your life!'" Whereupon Benny replied, "I'm thinking. I'm thinking."

Self-effacing humor even saved Abraham Lincoln's life once when he was a young man. While walking along a path through the woods, he came face to face with a rugged mountain man. The man pulled out his pistol and aimed it at Lincoln.

"I promised my mother," the man said, "that if'n I ever met a man that was uglier than me, I'd shoot him on the spot."

"Well, sir," said Lincoln, "if I really *am* uglier than you, I don't believe I would *want* to keep on living."

The mountain man broke into laughter and put the pistol away.

Try your hand occasionally at a few funny comments about yourself. Keep them brief, not more than four or five lines, and try them out on your family or close friends. Now and then, slip one into a normal conversation. *Don't* say, "Listen to this joke and tell me what you think." Just try the line on a few different people. If it works, keep it; if not, dump it. Either way, come back another time and work out a few more.

Self-effacing humor is useful as long as you don't overdo it. Don't put yourself down to the point that you seem neurotic and insecure, always demeaning yourself or fishing for reinforcement and validation. Your objective is not to be the court jester, but to humanize yourself in the eyes of others, who then will yield to the natural tendency of wanting to support and help someone who is "just a regular person like me."

Putting Some Punch Into Your Parlance

To get some first-hand experience with setups, punch lines, and exaggeration, play around with the following starters (remember to go for the jocular vein):

1. What if _____

_____

_____

_____

Example: What if Mr. Rogers were President? He'd probably convince the Democrats and Republicans to stop arguing and share some nice milk and graham crackers.

2. Have you ever noticed _____

_____

_____

3. Have you ever wondered why _____

_____

_____

4. Why is it that _____

_____

_____

5. What is it about _____

_____

_____

6. If I were <u>(name of famous person)</u>, I think I would ____

_____

_____

7. What really scares me is _____

_____

_____

8. I like to think of myself as _____

_____

_____

Chapter Five

Although your sense of humor didn't come with a set of instructions you can memorize, you may find the following points helpful and reassuring.

1. Don't feel like you have to tell jokes.

> "I read something funny in *Reader's Digest*. You know they have that section called 'Humor in Uniform'? Well, there was some Army guy, or maybe it was Navy, whatever. Anyway, this officer says ... no, actually it had to be Navy, because it was on a ship ... Anyway, he says ..."

Approaching life with humor doesn't mean you have to tell jokes. Some people aren't comfortable telling jokes, and some just don't do it very well. Nevertheless, if

you're drawn to this form of humor and really want to give it a try, here are some tips to keep in mind:

- When you hear a joke you think others will like, don't just try to remember it—write it down while it's fresh in your memory. Be sure you get it right.

- You may notice that the joke can be improved by using the techniques discussed earlier in this book. Perhaps the person who told you the joke didn't do it very well. Work on it, polish it, but be careful not to ruin it. Often even a slight change in wording can spoil a joke.

- Once you have the joke written and polished, memorize it. Do it exactly the way that gets the best laugh. Practice it until your timing and delivery are perfect, focusing on these points:

  Don't drag out the setup too long. Put pauses in where they strengthen the effect, but keep the story moving right along.

Don't telegraph the punch line. The element of surprise is an important component of the humor phenomenon.

Don't laugh while you are telling the joke (unless you are one of the very rare individuals, like Steve Allen, who has an infectious laugh that puts people in a good mood even before the joke is over).

• Ask yourself, "In what situations could I use this material? Where would this work?" Here's an example:

A minister moved into a small town and wanted to be of service in the community, so he applied to join the local business service club. The club secretary said, "There's one problem. Our club enrolls people by their occupation, and right now the category for clergy is all filled up. But we can still get you in if you don't mind being classed temporarily in another occupation."

The minister said, "Oh, that's fine with me. What category?"

The secretary looked in the book. "I'm sorry about this, but right now the only opening we have is in the category for 'Hog Callers.' Is that all right with you?"

The minister thought for a second and then said, "Well, in other places where I've labored, people usually referred to me as the shepherd of the flock. But then, I guess you know your members better than I do."

Where could you use this story? Obviously it would appeal to ministers and it would work at a meeting of a service club. It might even get a laugh from hog callers. In fact, you could probably tell it at any meeting that a clergy member opened. But there are other ways to take advantage of it. You could tell this story to illustrate one of several different points:

- Job titles aren't as important as doing your best at your job.

- If you truly want to be of service, you can put up with a temporary setback.

- Titles and job descriptions tend to stereotype people.

- Be careful how you label people; they may live up to the label.

Can you think of any others?

2. **Expect the unexpected.** Even Robin Williams, who is a great improviser, doesn't improvise everything—you just think he does. Consider your possibilities in advance, and be aware of planned spontaneity.

When a comedian breaks us up, we're usually too busy enjoying the routine to realize something: This comic has probably told the same jokes before in exactly the same way with precisely the same timing to dozens of audiences. Even if we do think of that, it doesn't matter. To us the humor seems fresh and original and, most important, it helps us relax.

Comedians aren't the only ones who do their homework, however. In preparing Ronald Reagan for the 1984 campaign debate, media consultant Roger Ailes asked the President what he would feel comfortable saying when the issue of his age inevitably arose. "Well," said Reagan, "there's a line I used to use..." and told Ailes the line. Ailes encouraged him to use it. During the debate, when Walter Mondale mentioned Reagan's age, Reagan replied: "I will not make age an issue in this campaign. I refuse to exploit for political purposes the youth and inexperience of my opponent." The entire audience laughed—even Walter Mondale.

This anticipating and strategizing is common for many of the quips, quick retorts, and ad libs you hear every day. Professional speakers, politicians, and performers who are often in front of audiences know there's always a chance something unplanned will happen. So they plan for it. People drop things, loud noises surprise us, equipment breaks at inopportune moments. Professionals know these things will happen eventually, so they prepare "recovery lines" (or "cover" lines) that they can use when the expected unexpected happens.

As the anecdote above shows, not all of Ronald Reagan's quick comebacks were impromptu. He often had a backup line to supplement his natual wit, and sometimes used professional writers such as Doug Gamble, who has written for Bob Hope, Joan Rivers, and others. Writing out a recovery line in advance is not cheating, it's not unfair, and it's not just politics. Many top executives do the same thing. It makes good business sense to be prepared, so you can regain your own composure quickly or perhaps ease someone else's moment of distress with poise.

Recovery lines don't have to be uproariously funny. When the podium falls off the stage or someone delivering sandwiches walks in on your big presentation, no one expects you to be brilliantly witty. The mere fact that you have the self-assurance to handle an unexpected development is a pleasant surprise. That you handle it with humor becomes a truly impressive bonus. It doesn't matter if your offhand remark would produce only a faint smile under ordinary circumstances. You win points just by having fun with something that would make most people feel embarrassed, defensive, or apologetic. In this way, you give your audience permission to empathize with your plight, but without having to feel embarrassed for you. And they'll love you for that.

Here are some examples of prepared recovery lines for a few common situations.

- *During an important meeting, you drop some papers.* "No wonder I can't hold on to this: it's printed on that new Teflon paper. Even the ink slides off." Or, "No wonder it's so slippery. This is the annual report from the WD-40 Company."

- *While you're showing a visitor around your department, you notice that you have an important button or zipper unfastened.* "Sorry about that. Serves me right for trying to get dressed and run down the street after my car pool at the same time."

- *As you're giving a luncheon speech, a waiter drops a tray of dishes.* "It's okay, folks. I paid the hotel to have that happen. I'll do anything to keep my audience awake."

- *Or the lights go off.* "Everybody please stay in your seats and relax for a minute while I write out a check to the electric company."

- *Or you stumble on your way up to the podium.* "Do you think the IRS will let me deduct that as a business trip?"

- *While you're making a presentation, you're asked a hostile question.* "I'm always glad to get questions like that. It gives me a chance to find out if my antiperspirant is really working."

Tapping the Humor Potential Around You

Using the familiar occurrences mentioned previously or others that you can think of, rough out at least one recovery line for each situation. Memorize the lines and practice them until they sound natural. Then relax and wait for the unexpected to happen. It will.

3. **Develop your own identity.** When you work from a
   persona that fits you, your humor will be more
   appropriate as well as more effective. If you are
   comfortable with your style of humor, your audience in
   turn will be comfortable with you. When your style
   faithfully expresses your personality, your appearance,
   and your background, you'll be funnier—and safer—
   than you would be joking about playing polo with the
   Prince of Wales or landing an F-14 on an aircraft carrier.
   (Unless, of course, you happen to be a polo-playing
   jet ace.)

   One further note about persona: Your vocabulary
   should match your character. If people describe you
   with words such as "dignified," "reserved," or perhaps
   even "stately," then you should probably go along with
   that by not using slang very often and by avoiding
   profanity entirely. (Can you imagine Dick Cavett trying
   to do "Gomer Pyle's" routine?)

   On the other hand, if you strike people as "a good ol'
   boy" or "a real down-home gal," then you could be
   making a mistake if you try to behave like the Duke of
   Edinburgh at a state funeral. Political writer Molly Ivins
   has produced two successful books and hundreds of
   columns by being content to stay herself—an intelligent
   and astute observer with a Texas drawl and a whole
   corralful of homey expressions.

During the Watergate hearings, American TV viewers were enthralled by the wit and folksy wisdom of Senator Sam Ervin of North Carolina. What few realized was that "Senator Sam," a bona fide "country boy," received his law degree from Harvard and had graduated from that institution with highest honors. Ervin knew how to use his persona to the best effect to increase his stature and respect. He made a definite plus out of a rural background that some people might have considered a drawback in the glare of the limelight.

EXERCISE #6

Finding Humorous Topics in Your Daily Activities

Funny people are observant people. As you go about your job each day, take note of topics that seem appropriate for you to talk about. If you're a salesperson, for example, you might find humor in clients, quotas, and commissions. Let each topic also suggest subtopics—for instance, business travel should suggest things like suitcases, hotels, rental cars, restaurants, airports, freeways, getting lost, feeling lonely, tipping people, meeting strange people, and on and on. Every one of these has been the focus of wit for more than one humorist. Now it's your turn. Make as long a list as you like, but remember to be true to your own style and identity.

_____

_____

_____

_____

_____

_____

_____

_____

_____

_____

4. **Get others to identify with the premise.** You develop a bond with your listeners by building on shared experiences and feelings, so offer them something they can identify with. What do you hate? It's likely others feel the same way. What do you have trouble with? Other people probably have had the very same problem. What is it that makes you feel inadequate, incompetent, ineffective, or inept? Whatever it is, you're sure to have lots of company. What really bugs you? What do you wonder or worry about? Develop a funny way to express it and people will relate to your experience:

> "You know what I wonder about: Why is it they never put smoke alarms inside elevators? Think about it—if you were in an elevator, wouldn't you want to know if the carpet was on fire?"

A word of warning: Don't try too hard. If smiles aren't spreading and eyes aren't twinkling, don't push your luck. Quit while you're ahead. Perhaps your timing is a little off, or possibly there's some serious undercurrent in the group that you aren't aware of that's keeping people from relaxing. Or maybe you just happened to get stuck this time in a room full of pompous, uptight fuddy-duddies who think "we important grown-ups don't have time for childish things like laughing." Hey, it happens.

Be sensitive to other people's moods. Never *try* to be funny when another person is having a problem, unless he or she seems willing to laugh at the problem too. When the computer is down and a co-worker is terrified about losing important data, that's probably not a good time to start joking about seeing smoke and sparks coming out of the hard drive!

If you see your humor isn't working, back off immediately. There will be other times. Being sensitive to your audience is the *one* overriding principle in humor, in performance, in presentation, or for that matter, in any form of human communication. It bears repeating: *Be sensitive to other people.*

EXERCISE #7

Identifying Common Experiences That Have Humor Potential

To help yourself tap the "humor potential" around you, make the following lists:

10 Things That Really Bug Me

_____

_____

_____

_____

_____

_____

_____

_____

_____

_____

10 Ways I Feel Inadequate

_____

_____

_____

_____

_____

_____

_____

_____

_____

10 Things I Wonder About

_____

_____

_____

_____

_____

_____

_____

_____

_____

_____

Here's a variation: What are you proud of that you can make fun of?

> "You know what I'm really proud of? I'm the only person in this company who doesn't foul things up when I take sick leave. In fact, the longer I'm out sick, the better my department seems to run."

10 Things I'm Proud Of

_____

_____

_____

_____

_____

_____

_____

_____

_____

_____

Chapter Six

Risky Humor: What to Avoid

In a Supreme Court case, Justice Potter Stewart said although he couldn't define obscenity, "I know it when I see it." The same could be said about inappropriate humor. It's difficult to define, but if we are the least bit sensitive to the feelings of others, we know unsuitable humor when we hear it. It is humor that offends any listeners for any reason, particularly if it shocks or embarrasses them.

The broadest definition would be that any humor is unsuitable if your listener doesn't laugh at it. The keystone of humor is to know your audience. If you have any reason to suspect that something might upset your listeners, drop it from your repertory. Your purpose in using humor at work isn't to make you the next George Carlin or Judy Tenuta—it's to help you be happy and successful in the business world.

Even if it isn't your intention to offend anyone, unsuitable humor has definite, often lasting, effects. It undermines people's self-confidence and pushes you outside of that important humor/trust circle discussed earlier. Offensive humor makes a major withdrawal from the goodwill account you have built up with your colleagues.

Unsuitable humor can also get you into serious legal problems: It is listed as a form of harassment by the Equal Employment Opportunity Commission (EEOC). Many companies now have clearly defined rules concerning what to do if someone is using racist, ethnic, or sexist humor. Ask your supervisor for details. If your company doesn't already have such a policy, it should develop one.

Another reason not to use inappropriate humor is that it has an alienating effect. It can cause colleagues to feel as if they're outside the circle and perhaps to doubt themselves—Will the others still like me if I don't laugh at this? Will they think I'm old-fashioned and square? Will they tell jokes about *me* when

I'm not here? Are they just testing me to see if I can take it? Am I just being oversensitive? Maybe there's something wrong with my sense of humor.

Group Stereotypes

The most common types of inappropriate humor are ethnic, racial, or national. This sort of humor derives from stereotypes: characteristics, generally negative, that supposedly are common to most or all members of a particular group. Often the same joke travels around the world, changing its reference point as it crosses boundaries. The Germans tell it about the Italians; the British tell it about the French. New Yorkers will quip "Did you hear the one about the guy from Los Angeles?" while people in L.A. are asking "Did you hear the one about the guy from Hollywood?" (And people in Hollywood say, "Have your secretary phone my secretary—I have a great joke for you.")

As a general rule, don't even attempt ethnic or national humor. There is absolutely ZERO to be gained from giving others the idea that you have a prejudiced streak. To think (or give the impression that you think) every individual in a group has the same personality, habits, and traits shows a basic insensitivity to the wondrous variety of human beings. There are only a couple of exceptions to this rule:

1. **The humor must be about your own ethnic group or nationality.** Yakov Smirnoff does a funny job of comparing life in the U.S. with life in his native Russia. He does it so well, in fact, that most people don't know (and don't care) that he hasn't lived there for many years. In the same vein, Richard Pryor, Eddie Murphy, Roseanne Katon, George Wallace, and Marsha Warfield can all joke about being African-American because that's what they are.

2. Personalize the humor as much as possible. You can defuse the negative elements if you talk about a specific person, preferably a relative, rather than a generic stereotype. Don't say, "Once there was an old Scotsman, and you know how tight they are with their money ..." Instead, say, "My Great-Uncle Angus was very, very careful with his money. Maybe you've heard of him—he and another Scot invented copper wire when they both saw a penny on the sidewalk at the same time."

By connecting the joke with your own family tree, you give the humor an element of self-deprecation, as well as a certain amount of affection.

This connection is usually enough to neutralize the offensive element—the impression that you are attacking others unfairly. Hal Roach can launch barbs at the Irish; Allan Fotheringham can zing Canadians. They can do it, get away with it, and be loved for it because they belong.

Avoid sexist humor. James Thurber was famous for his "war between the sexes" cartoons, and Gracie Allen played perhaps the funniest, and dumbest, wife on radio and television. But those were different times. Today, no matter how funny you think a "dumb blond" or "silly housewife" joke is, pass it up. If you happen to be a blond or a housewife, or for that matter a blond housewife, pass it up anyway. You are bound to offend someone, and not just women; many men are also sensitive to anti-female humor.

Never make fun of other people's religion. If it's your own faith, well—see tips 1 and 2 mentioned earlier in this section. Richard Lewis can "do Jewish" because he is Jewish, and proud of it. If it weren't for Woody Allen's stereotyped neurotic, intellectual, New York Jewish character, he might still be an unknown gag-writer for television shows. Dave Markwell and Calvin Grondahl can be funny about Mormonism because they are both of that faith. But when a famous non-LDS comedienne tried to zing the Mormons, she bombed. People won't respect you if they feel you're attacking someone else's sacred beliefs. And they won't laugh!

Physical shortcomings present another area where you should tread lightly, if at all. Katherine Buckley jokes about her hearing disability. Geri Jewell has developed her entire routine around the fact that she has cerebral palsy. Danny Thomas and Jimmy Durante could do nose shtick, and Mickey Rooney can tell short-people jokes. But if you're not your own victim, stay clear of the area.

Okay, no disability jokes. Then what about someone who is nerdy, awkward, or shaped like an overstuffed laundry bag? Is that person fair game? Only if you are that someone, and only if you feel comfortable poking fun at your own physical imperfections. Bear one other thing in mind: Can you keep control of the situation? If other people think your self-directed jokes give them permission to join in and start teasing you about your waistline, hairline, and facial lines, will you still be thinking, "Hey, now that's funny stuff"? If you're not really, *really* self-assured, then you'd better save your physical references for the comedy club, where you have control of the microphone and can walk away when you choose.

A final thought about group stereotypes: Never assume you're safe in using ethnic, nationalist, racist, or sexist humor just because your listener doesn't belong to those groups. An Asian woman may be offended by anti-Polish jokes; you never know what people's sensitivities are, so just don't do it.

Sarcasm

You can also be on dangerous ground with certain other types of humor, such as sarcasm. Sarcasm is humor that is contemptuous, mocking, taunting or, as one dictionary puts it, "marked by the intent to wound." Sarcasm is an attempt to get laughs through the use of ridicule. As in fencing, you score only by landing the point of the blade on another person. In the business world, people often aim sarcastic remarks at the company itself or at the policies instituted by company leaders. This can quickly destroy a happy, cooperative atmosphere in your workplace.

Sarcasm is hurtful, negative, and should generally be avoided. However, there is one form that can be funny, provided you don't aim it at people or your organization. You can often make something humorous by saying you love it when actually you hate it:

> "You know what I really love about Friday afternoons? It's knowing that no matter what time I get on the freeway, there will be fifteen thousand other cars that got there just two minutes ahead of me. I mean, what happens here? When I walk into the elevator, does somebody wave a checkered flag out the window to let all the people in the parking lot know it's time to start their engines?"

"Playful" Insults

Close on the risk scale to sarcasm are mock insults. Co-workers often enjoy indulging in a battle of wits, each trying to top the other in thinking up clever jibes. This is especially true with men, who perhaps subconsciously think of mutual insults as a form of friendly competition. Since we no longer grab swords and armor and head for the ramparts, these "zingers" act as a substitute for the physical combat that's no longer an acceptable way of doing business. (That is, unless your occupation happens to be NFL lineman.)

If no one takes the banter seriously, and everyone involved enjoys it, such humor can strengthen the bond between colleagues. In order for people to tacitly consent to let each other "take their best shot," a certain level of trust is necessary. Mock insults at the same time validate that the atmosphere of trust exists. Such play can be a positive team-building technique, but only if it is enjoyed by everyone and only if kept within reasonable bounds.

After a plane crash, one survivor reported that he had kept calm by reading a novel by Arthur C. Clarke. When this was printed in the newspapers, Clarke sent a copy of the article to his friendly rival Isaac Asimov. At the bottom he wrote, "What a pity he didn't read one of your novels. He would have slept through the whole wretched ordeal."

"On the contrary," Asimov wrote back, "the reason he was reading your novel was that if the plane did crash, death would come as a blessed release."

It's not difficult to picture these two highly intelligent and literate colleagues enjoying their lifelong relationship of mutual heckling. However, not everyone is willing to play that kind of game. Don't indulge in it unless you know the other person very well, and your relationship is such that both of you feel comfortable with "slams" and "put-downs." If there's any question that you may offend your partner, then it doesn't matter how witty you think your wisecrack will be—pass it up.

Practical Jokes

"When in doubt—don't!" also applies strongly to pranks, practical jokes, and hoaxes. The problem with these forms of humor is that usually some element is intended to cause embarrassment, humiliation, emotional distress, or even physical pain. Some practical jokes can get out of control and be downright dangerous.

For example, maybe you think it would be really funny to hand Fred his coffee in a dribble cup and watch his response when he realizes a trail of liquid is running down the middle of his necktie. Well, maybe. But what if it's a brand-new tie, an expensive one at that, and it was a gift from his 12-year-old daughter who babysat for sixteen hours to get enough money to buy it? What now, Groucho? Still think it's funny?

For practical jokes and hoaxes, the bottom line is this: Will the victim laugh with you? Does the prank bring everyone together in a spirit of camaraderie? When it's over, will the victim feel like slapping you on the back, or belting you in the mouth?

"Off-Color" Humor

There's one more entry on the list of humor "don'ts": You don't have to be dirty to get laughs. True, people do laugh when they hear "blue" humor, but it's often because we tend to laugh nervously when we're embarrassed, especially in the company of people we don't know very well. Be honest about any such risky humor you're tempted to use at work. If you took out all the four-letter words and bathroom humor, would people still laugh? If the answer is "no," that should tell you something about the quality of the humor. If the material is funny, it will still be funny without the dirty parts, and you won't have to worry about offending someone.

In short, with all your attempts to make people laugh, ask yourself: Is it harmless, helpful, and benign? Will it dispel tension, clear the air, and help us all to relax and work together? Or is it venomous, poisoning our attitudes and shriveling our enthusiasm? Does it tear people down, or build them up?

Irony is a form of expression in which the meaning that is intended is in direct opposition to its usual sense. Irony is often used to point out the incongruity and absurdities of human existence. You know Parkinson's Law ("A task will expand to fill the amount of time allotted to it"), and you've heard lots of Murphy's Laws ("If anything can go wrong, it will"). Now try your hand at writing your own laws. Here are a few ideas to get you started.

- The time it takes to get approval for a project is 1.8 times the total ages of all the supervisors who have to approve it.

- The person who left you an "Urgent—phone me immediately" message only three minutes ago will have "just stepped out for lunch" when you phone right back.

- When you need just one more copy and there's only one piece of paper left in the copier, it will jam and get torn in half.

- When you drive the old heap with the stuck front door and the big smelly spot where the baby threw up on the passenger seat, that's the day your boss will ask you to go pick up a client at the airport.

(fill in your name)'s Laws

_____

_____

_____

_____

Chapter 7

On his deathbed, the popular 19th-century actor Edmund Kean uttered these famous last words: "Dying is easy; comedy is hard."

If you're ready to claim your share of the many benefits of humor, you'll have to be willing to put out a certain amount of effort. If you haven't completed all the exercises in this book, make time to do so. If you've worked through them all, then be sure to do them again, in any order you like. Plan to tackle at least one exercise a week, and spend at least 30 minutes every other day polishing your comedic skills.

Many people have learned to use humor to their advantage in the business world, and you can too. If you're ready to spread some cheer in an often dreary world and help others enjoy life more while you're passing through it, get to work having fun and you'll soon be having fun at work.

EXERCISE #9

The Last (and Best) Exercise

The next time you're consumed by problems at work and tempted to think your job is the sum total of existence, do the following: Check out some joke or riddle books from the children's department at the library and take them to the nearest children's hospital. Volunteer to spend an hour or two reading to the kids. You'll bring smiles to a very appreciative audience and put some twinkle back into your own eyes!

It's amazing how small our own problems seem when we look at them through laughing eyes.

Bibliography

Allen, Steven. *Make 'em Laugh*. Buffalo, NY: Promethus Books, 1993.

Basso, Bob. *This Job Should Be Fun*. Holbrook, MA: Bob Adams, 1991.

Cousins, Norman. *Anatomy of an Illness as Perceived by the Patient: Reflections on Healing and Recognition*. Toronto: Bantam, 1981.

Fagan, Pete, and Mark Schaffer. *The Office Humor Book*. New York: Brown Publishing Group, 1984.

Gardner, Dianne. *Gender Quotes*. Del Mar, CA: Qualified Insights Press, 1994.

Harris, Sidney. *What's So Funny About Business? Yuppies, Bosses, and Other Capitalists*. Los Altos, CA: W. Kaufmann, 1986.

Klein, Allen. *The Healing Power of Humor: Techniques on Getting Through Loss, Setbacks, Upsets, Disappointments, Difficulties, Trials, Tribulations, and All That Not-So-Funny Stuff*. Los Angeles: J.P. Tarcher, 1989.

Kushner, Malcolm. *The Light Touch: How to Use Humor for Business Success*. New York: Simon and Schuster, 1990.

Ross, Bob. *Laugh, Lead, and Profit: Building Productive Workplaces With Humor*. San Diego, CA: Arrowhead, 1989.

Self-Study Sourcebooks

Climbing the Corporate Ladder: What You Need to Know and Do to Be a Promotable Person *by Barbara Pachter and Marjorie Brody*

Coping With Supervisory Nightmares: 12 Common Nightmares of Leadership and What You Can Do About Them *by Michael and Deborah Singer Dobson*

Defeating Procrastination: 52 Fail-Safe Tips for Keeping Time on Your Side *by Marlene Caroselli, Ed.D.*

Discovering Your Purpose *by Ivy Haley*

Going for the Gold: Winning the Gold Medal for Financial Independence *by Lesley D. Bissett, CFP*

Having Something to Say When You Have to Say Something: The Art of Organizing Your Presentation *by Randy Horn*

Info-Flood: How to Swim in a Sea of Information Without Going Under *by Marlene Caroselli, Ed.D.*

The Innovative Secretary *by Marlene Caroselli, Ed.D.*

Mastering the Art of Communication: Your Keys to Developing a More Effective Personal Style *by Michelle Fairfield Poley*

Obstacle Illusions: Coverting Crisis to Opportunity *by Marlene Caroselli, Ed.D.*

Organized for Success! 95 Tips for Taking Control of Your Time, Your Space, and Your Life *by Nanci McGraw*

A Passion to Lead! How to Develop Your Natural Leadership Ability *by Michael Plumstead*

P.E.R.S.U.A.D.E.: Communication Strategies That Move People to Action *by Marlene Caroselli, Ed.D.*

Productivity Power: 250 Great Ideas for Being More Productive *by Jim Temme*

Promoting Yourself: 50 Ways to Increase Your Prestige, Power, and Paycheck *by Marlene Caroselli, Ed.D.*

Proof Positive: How to Find Errors Before They Embarrass You *by Karen L. Anderson*

Risk-Taking: 50 Ways to Turn Risks Into Rewards *by Marlene Caroselli, Ed.D. and David Harris*

Stress Control: How You Can Find Relief From Life's Daily Stress *by Steve Bell*

The Technical Writer's Guide *by Robert McGraw*

Total Quality Customer Service: How to Make It Your Way of Life *by Jim Temme*

Write It Right! A Guide for Clear and Correct Writing *by Richard Andersen and Helene Hinis*

Your Total Communication Image *by Janet Signe Olson, Ph.D.*

Handbooks

The ABC's of Empowered Teams: Building Blocks for Success *by Mark Towers*

Assert Yourself! Developing Power-Packed Communication Skills to Make Your Points
  Clearly, Confidently, and Persuasively *by Lisa Contini*
Breaking the Ice: How to Improve Your On-the-Spot Communication Skills
  by Deborah Shouse
The Care and Keeping of Customers: A Treasury of Facts, Tips, and Proven
  Techniques for Keeping Your Customers Coming BACK! *by Roy Lantz*
Challenging Change: Five Steps for Dealing With Change *by Holly DeForest and
  Mary Steinberg*
Dynamic Delegation: A Manager's Guide for Active Empowerment *by Mark Towers*
Every Woman's Guide to Career Success *by Denise M. Dudley*
Grammar? No Problem! *by Dave Davies*
Great Openings and Closings: 28 Ways to Launch and Land Your Presentations With
  Punch, Power, and Pizazz *by Mari Pat Varga*
Hiring and Firing: What Every Manager Needs to Know *by Marlene Caroselli, Ed.D.
  with Laura Wyeth, Ms.Ed.*
How to Be a More Effective Group Communicator: Finding Your Role and Boosting
  Your Confidence in Group Situations *by Deborah Shouse*
How to Deal With Difficult People *by Paul Friedman*
Learning to Laugh at Work: The Power of Humor in the Workplace
  by Robert McGraw
Making Your Mark: How to Develop a Personal Marketing Plan for Becoming More
  Visible and More Appreciated at Work *by Deborah Shouse*
Meetings That Work *by Marlene Caroselli, Ed.D.*
The Mentoring Advantage: How to Help Your Career Soar to New Heights
  by Pam Grout
Minding Your Business Manners: Etiquette Tips for Presenting Yourself Professionally
  in Every Business Situation *by Marjorie Brody and Barbara Pachter*
Misspeller's Guide *by Joel and Ruth Schroeder*
Motivation in the Workplace: How to Motivate Workers to Peak Performance and
  Productivity *by Barbara Fielder*
NameTags Plus: Games You Can Play When People Don't Know What to Say
  by Deborah Shouse
Networking: How to Creatively Tap Your People Resources *by Colleen Clarke*
New & Improved! 25 Ways to Be More Creative and More Effective *by Pam Grout*
Power Write! A Practical Guide to Words That Work *by Helene Hinis*
The Power of Positivity: Eighty ways to energize your life
  by Joel and Ruth Schroeder
Putting Anger to Work For You *by Ruth and Joel Schroeder*
Reinventing Your Self: 28 Strategies for Coping With Change *by Mark Towers*
Saying "No" to Negativity: How to Manage Negativity in Yourself, Your Boss, and
  Your Co-Workers *by Zoie Kaye*
The Supervisor's Guide: The Everyday Guide to Coordinating People and Tasks
  by Jerry Brown and Denise Dudley, Ph.D.
Taking Charge: A Personal Guide to Managing Projects and Priorities
  by Michal E. Feder
Treasure Hunt: 10 Stepping Stones to a New and More Confident You!
  by Pam Grout
A Winning Attitude: How to Develop Your Most Important Asset!
  by Michelle Fairfield Poley

For more information, call 1-800-873-7545.

Notes

Notes